easy
Pasta

easy
Pasta

LOVE FOOD

Love Food ® is an imprint of Parragon Books Ltd

Parragon
Queen Street House
4 Queen Street
Bath BA1 1HE, UK

Photography by Günter Beer and Don Last
Food Styling by Oliver Trific and Christine France
Introduction by Anne Sheasby

ISBN: 978-1-4075-6792-1

Printed in Indonesia

NOTES FOR THE READER

- This book uses imperial, metric, and US cup measurements. Follow the same units of measurement throughout; do not mix imperial and metric.
- All spoon measurements are level: teaspoons are assumed to be 5 ml, and tablespoons are assumed to be 15 ml.
- Unless otherwise stated, milk is assumed to be lowfat and eggs are medium. The times given are an approximate guide only.
- Some recipes contain nuts. If you are allergic to nuts you should avoid using them and any products containing nuts.
- Recipes using raw or very lightly cooked eggs should be avoided by infants, the elderly, pregnant women, convalescents, and anyone with a chronic condition.

Contents

	Introduction	6
1	Soups & Salads	8
2	Meat & Poultry	46
3	Fish & Seafood	84
4	Vegetarian	122
	Index	160

Introduction

Pasta has played an important role in the Italian diet for centuries, but it has also become a very popular food in many countries across the globe. Pasta is a versatile, convenient, and economical food. It is easy to prepare, quick to cook, and can be combined with all sorts of ingredients to create a tempting range of dishes to suit all tastes.

The word pasta literally means "dough" or "paste." The best fresh pastas are made from a basic combination of type/grade "00" pasta flour, eggs, salt, and sometimes a little olive oil and/or water. Top-quality dried pastas are made from 100 percent durum (hard, high-protein) wheat, and some include the addition of eggs. Other ingredients, such as spinach, garlic, chopped herbs, tomato paste, squid ink, mushrooms, beet, saffron, etc, may be added to the basic pasta dough for extra flavor and color.

The variety of both fresh and dried pastas available is extensive and includes long pasta (such as spaghetti, tagliatelle, and linguine), short pasta (such as penne, macaroni, and fusilli) or more unusual shapes (such as conchiglie, radiatori, or lumache). Other varieties include soup pasta (pastina or "little pasta") and filled pasta such as ravioli. Lasagna sheets and cannelloni tubes are used in baked pasta dishes.

Storing Pasta

Dried pasta is a convenient pantry standby as it has a long shelf life. Dried pasta should be stored in an airtight container in a cool, dry place. Keep an eye on the "best before" date on the packaging.

Fresh pasta on the other hand is best used immediately or stored in an airtight container in the refrigerator and used within 2 days. Cooled cooked pasta should be kept in a sealed container in the refrigerator and used within 2 days.

Plain cooked pasta does not freeze well on its own, but it does freeze successfully in dishes such as lasagna. Uncooked fresh pasta freezes well in a covered container or sealed plastic freezer bag for up to 1 month and it can be cooked from frozen.

Cooking Pasta

Pasta should always be cooked in a large pan containing plenty of salted boiling water. It should be added to fast-boiling water and the water should be kept at a rolling boil throughout cooking. Stir the pasta when you initially add it to the water, then quickly bring it to a boil again, and continue to cook the pasta uncovered, stirring occasionally.

You can add a dash of oil to the cooking water if you wish. Some believe that the addition of oil helps to prevent the pasta from sticking together, but it is not strictly necessary.

Fresh unfilled pasta takes 1–3 minutes to cook and fresh filled pasta takes 3–4 minutes to cook, depending on the variety. Dried unfilled pasta takes 8–10 minutes to cook, and dried filled pasta takes 10–15 minutes to cook, depending on the variety.

Cooked pasta should be "al dente" which means that it should be tender but still have a slight resistance to the bite. As soon as the pasta is cooked, drain it thoroughly through a colander or large strainer, shaking off any excess water, then quickly toss it with the prepared sauce or ingredients. Serve the hot pasta immediately on warmed plates or in warmed bowls.

If you are serving the cooked pasta cold, for example in a pasta salad, rinse the pasta under cold running water to stop any further cooking, then drain it well. Toss the cold pasta with a little olive oil or salad dressing to prevent the pieces sticking together, then chill until required.

Serving Pasta

Choosing which pasta to serve with a particular sauce is often a matter of personal taste but the following general guidelines may help.

Small pasta tubes and twists, such as penne (quills), farfalle (bows), and fusilli (spirals), are ideal for chunky vegetable sauces and some meat or cream-based sauces. Larger pasta tubes, such as rigatoni, are good for some meat sauces.

Smooth-textured sauces based on cream, butter, or olive oil are ideal for long strands of pasta, such as spaghetti, tagliatelle, linguine, or fettucine. The sauce should be able to cling to the long pasta when it is twirled onto a fork.

Pasta such as lasagna, cannelloni, and macaroni work best when baked in recipes.

The smallest pasta shapes are ideal for adding texture and interest to soups.

1

Soups & Salads

Minestrone

serves 4

- 2 tbsp olive oil
- 2 garlic cloves, chopped
- 2 red onions, chopped
- 2¾ oz/75 g prosciutto, sliced
- 1 red bell pepper, seeded and chopped
- 1 orange bell pepper, seeded and chopped
- 14 oz/400 g canned chopped tomatoes
- 4 cups vegetable stock
- 1 celery stalk, trimmed and sliced
- 14 oz/400 g canned cranberry beans, drained
- 3½ oz/100 g green leafy cabbage, shredded
- 2¾ oz/75 g frozen peas, thawed
- 1 tbsp chopped fresh flat-leaf parsley
- 2¾ oz/75 g dried vermicelli
- salt and pepper
- freshly grated Parmesan cheese, to garnish

Heat the oil in a large pan. Add the garlic, onions, and prosciutto and cook over medium heat, stirring, for 3 minutes, until slightly softened. Add the red and orange bell peppers and the chopped tomatoes and cook for an additional 2 minutes, stirring. Stir in the stock, then add the celery, cranberry beans, cabbage, peas, and parsley. Season to taste with salt and pepper. Bring to a boil, then lower the heat and simmer for 30 minutes.

Add the vermicelli to the pan. Cook for another 4–5 minutes, or according to the instructions on the package. Remove from the heat and ladle into warmed serving bowls. Garnish with freshly grated Parmesan and serve immediately.

Brown Lentil & Pasta Soup

serves 4

- 4 strips lean bacon, cut into small squares
- 1 onion, chopped
- 2 garlic cloves, crushed
- 2 celery stalks, chopped
- 1¾ oz/50 g dried farfallini (small pasta bows)
- 14 oz/400 g canned brown lentils, drained
- 5 cups vegetable stock
- 2 tbsp chopped fresh mint, plus extra sprigs to garnish

Place the bacon in a large skillet together with the onion, garlic, and celery. Cook for 4–5 minutes, stirring, until the onion is tender and the bacon is just beginning to brown.

Add the pasta to the skillet and cook, stirring, for 1 minute to coat the pasta in the fat.

Add the lentils and the stock, and bring to a boil. Reduce the heat and simmer for 8–10 minutes, or until the pasta is tender but still firm to the bite.

Remove the skillet from the heat and stir in the chopped fresh mint. Transfer to warmed serving bowls, garnish with fresh mint sprigs, and serve immediately.

Tuscan Bean Soup

serves 6

10½ oz/300 g canned cannellini beans, drained and rinsed

10½ oz/300 g canned cranberry beans, drained and rinsed

about 2½ cups chicken or vegetable stock

4 oz/115 g dried macaroni (small pasta shells)

4–5 tbsp olive oil

2 garlic cloves, very finely chopped

3 tbsp chopped fresh flat-leaf parsley

salt and pepper

Place half the cannellini and half the cranberry beans in a food processor with half the stock and process until smooth. Pour into a large, heavy-bottom pan and add the remaining beans. Stir in enough of the remaining stock to achieve the consistency you like, then bring to a boil.

Add the pasta and return to a boil, then reduce the heat and cook for 8–10 minutes, or until just tender.

Meanwhile, heat 3 tablespoons of the oil in a small skillet. Add the garlic and cook, stirring constantly, for 2–3 minutes, or until golden. Stir the garlic into the soup with the parsley.

Season to taste with salt and pepper and ladle into warmed serving bowls. Drizzle with the remaining olive oil to taste and serve immediately.

Potato & Pesto Soup

serves 4

2 tbsp olive oil

3 strips smoked, fatty bacon, chopped

2 tbsp butter

1 lb/450 g mealy potatoes, finely chopped

1 lb/450 g onions, finely chopped

2½ cups chicken stock

2½ cups milk

3½ oz/100 g dried conchigliette (small pasta shells)

⅔ cup heavy cream

2 tbsp pesto

2 tbsp chopped fresh flat-leaf parsley

salt and pepper

shavings of fresh Parmesan, to serve

Heat the oil in a large saucepan and cook the bacon over medium heat for 4 minutes. Add the butter, potatoes, and onions, and cook for 12 minutes, stirring constantly.

Add the stock and milk to the pan, bring to a boil, and simmer for 5 minutes. Add the pasta and simmer for an additional 3–5 minutes.

Blend in the cream and simmer for 5 minutes. Add the pesto and chopped parsley and season to taste with salt and pepper. Transfer the soup to warmed serving bowls and serve with Parmesan cheese.

Fresh Tomato Soup

serves 4

1 tbsp olive oil

1 lb 7 oz/650 g plum tomatoes

1 onion, cut into quarters

1 garlic clove, sliced thinly

1 celery stalk, roughly chopped

generous 2 cups chicken stock

2 oz/55 g dried anellini or other soup pasta

salt and pepper

chopped fresh flat-leaf parsley, to garnish

Heat the oil in a large, heavy-bottom pan and add the tomatoes, onion, garlic, and celery. Cover and cook over low heat for 45 minutes, occasionally shaking the pan gently, until the mixture is pulpy.

Transfer the mixture to a food processor or blender and process to a smooth purée. Push the purée through a strainer into a clean pan.

Add the stock and bring to a boil. Add the pasta, bring back to a boil and cook for 8–10 minutes, until the pasta is tender but still firm to the bite. Season to taste with salt and pepper. Ladle into warmed serving bowls, sprinkle with the parsley, and serve immediately.

Italian Chicken Soup

serves 4

1 lb/450 g skinless, boneless chicken breast, cut into thin strips

5 cups chicken stock

⅔ cup heavy cream

4 oz/115 g dried vermicelli

1 tbsp cornstarch

3 tbsp milk

6 oz/175 g canned corn kernels, drained

salt and pepper

Place the chicken in a large pan and pour in the chicken stock and cream. Bring to a boil, then reduce the heat and let simmer for 20 minutes.

Meanwhile, bring a large heavy-bottom pan of lightly salted water to a boil. Add the pasta, return to a boil, and cook for 8–10 minutes, or until just tender but still firm to the bite. Drain the pasta well and keep warm.

Season the soup to taste with salt and pepper. Mix the cornstarch and milk together until a smooth paste forms, then stir it into the soup. Add the corn and pasta and heat through. Ladle into warmed serving bowls and serve.

Chicken & Bean Soup

serves 4

2 tbsp butter

3 scallions, chopped

2 garlic cloves, finely chopped

1 fresh marjoram sprig, finely chopped

12 oz/350 g boneless chicken breasts, diced

5 cups chicken stock

12 oz/350 g canned chickpeas, drained and rinsed

1 bouquet garni

1 red bell pepper, diced

1 green bell pepper, diced

4 oz/115 g dried macaroni

salt and white pepper

croutons, to serve

Melt the butter in a large pan over medium heat. Add the scallions, garlic, marjoram, and chicken and cook, stirring frequently, for 5 minutes.

Add the stock, chickpeas, and bouquet garni, then season to taste with salt and white pepper.

Bring the soup to a boil over medium heat, then reduce the heat and simmer for about 2 hours.

Add the diced bell peppers and pasta to the pan, then simmer for an additional 20 minutes.

Ladle the soup into warmed serving bowls and sprinkle over the croutons. Serve immediately.

Tuscan Veal Broth

serves 4

- 1/3 cup dried peas, soaked for 2 hours and drained
- 2 lb/900 g boned neck of veal, diced
- 5 cups beef stock
- 2 1/2 cups water
- 1/3 cup pearl barley, washed
- 1 large carrot, diced
- 1 small turnip (about 6 oz/175 g), diced
- 1 large leek, thinly sliced
- 1 red onion, finely chopped
- 3 1/2 oz/100 g chopped tomatoes
- 1 fresh basil sprig
- 3 1/2 oz/100 g dried vermicelli
- salt and pepper

Put the peas, veal, stock, and water into a large pan and bring to a boil over low heat. Using a slotted spoon, skim off any foam that rises to the surface.

When all of the foam has been removed, add the pearl barley and a pinch of salt to the mixture. Simmer gently over low heat for 25 minutes.

Add the carrot, turnip, leek, onion, tomatoes, and basil to the pan, and season to taste with salt and pepper. Simmer for about 2 hours, skimming the surface from time to time to remove any foam. Remove the pan from the heat and set aside for 2 hours.

Set the pan over medium heat and bring to a boil. Add the vermicelli and cook for 8–10 minutes. Season to taste with salt and pepper, then remove and discard the basil. Ladle into warmed serving bowls and serve.

Fish Soup with Macaroni

serves 6

2 tbsp olive oil

2 onions, sliced

1 garlic clove, finely chopped

4 cups fish stock or water

14 oz/400 g canned chopped tomatoes

¼ tsp herbes de Provence

¼ tsp saffron threads

4 oz/115 g dried macaroni

18 live mussels, scrubbed and debearded

1 lb/450 g monkfish fillet, cut into chunks

8 oz/225 g raw shrimp, peeled and deveined, tails left on

salt and pepper

Heat the oil in a large, heavy-bottom pan. Add the onions and garlic and cook over low heat, stirring occasionally, for 5 minutes, or until the onions have softened.

Add the stock with the tomatoes and their can juices, herbs, saffron, and pasta, and season to taste with salt and pepper. Bring to a boil, then cover and simmer for 15 minutes.

Discard any mussels with broken shells or any that refuse to close when tapped. Add the mussels, monkfish, and shrimp to the pan. Re-cover and simmer for an additional 5–10 minutes, until the mussels have opened, the shrimp have changed color, and the fish is opaque and flakes easily. Discard any mussels that remain closed. Ladle the soup into warmed serving bowls and serve.

Warm Pasta Salad

serves 4

8 oz/225 g dried farfalle

6 pieces of sun-dried tomato in oil, drained and chopped

4 scallions, chopped

1¼ cups arugula, shredded

½ cucumber, seeded and diced

salt and pepper

freshly grated Parmesan cheese, to serve

for the dressing

4 tbsp olive oil

1 tbsp white wine vinegar

½ tsp superfine sugar

1 tsp whole grain mustard

salt and pepper

4 fresh basil leaves, finely shredded

To make the dressing, whisk the oil, vinegar, sugar, and mustard together in a bowl or pitcher. Season to taste with salt and pepper and stir in the basil.

Bring a large heavy-bottom pan of lightly salted water to a boil. Add the pasta, return to a boil, and cook for 8–10 minutes, or until tender but still firm to the bite. Drain and transfer to a salad bowl. Add the dressing and toss well.

Add the tomatoes, scallions, arugula, and cucumber, season to taste with salt and pepper, and toss. Sprinkle with the Parmesan cheese and serve warm.

Pasta Salad with Walnuts & Gorgonzola

serves 4

8 oz/225 g dried farfalle (pasta bows)

2 tbsp walnut oil

4 tbsp safflower oil

2 tbsp balsamic vinegar

10 oz/280 g mixed salad greens

8 oz/225 g Gorgonzola cheese, diced

½ cup walnuts, halved and toasted

salt and pepper

Bring a large, heavy-bottom pan of lightly salted water to a boil. Add the pasta, return to a boil, and cook for 8–10 minutes, or until tender but still firm to the bite. Drain and refresh in a bowl of cold water. Drain again.

Mix the walnut oil, safflower oil, and vinegar together in a bowl, whisking well, and season to taste with salt and pepper.

Arrange the salad greens in a large serving bowl. Top with the pasta, Gorgonzola cheese, and walnuts. Pour the dressing over the salad, toss lightly, and serve.

Penne & Apple Salad

serves 4

- 2 large heads of lettuce
- 9 oz/250 g dried penne (pasta quills)
- 1 tbsp olive oil
- 8 red apples
- juice of 4 lemons
- 1 stalk of celery, sliced
- 3/4 cup walnut halves
- 1 cup fresh garlic mayonnaise
- salt

Wash and drain the lettuce leaves, then pat them dry with paper towels. Transfer them to the refrigerator for 1 hour, until crisp.

Meanwhile, bring a large pan of lightly salted water to a boil. Add the pasta and olive oil, back bring to a boil, and cook for 8–10 minutes, or until tender but still firm to the bite. Drain the pasta and refresh under cold running water. Drain thoroughly and set aside.

Core and dice the apples, then place them in a small bowl and sprinkle with the lemon juice to coat them thoroughly – this will prevent them from turning brown. Mix together the pasta, celery, apples, and walnut halves and toss the mixture in the garlic mayonnaise. Add more mayonnaise, to taste.

Line a salad bowl with the lettuce leaves and spoon the pasta salad into the lined bowl. Refrigerate until ready to serve.

Pasta Salad with Bell Peppers

serves 4

1 red bell pepper

1 orange bell pepper

10 oz/280 g dried conchiglie (pasta shells)

5 tbsp extra virgin olive oil

2 tbsp lemon juice

2 tbsp pesto

1 garlic clove, very finely chopped

3 tbsp shredded fresh basil leaves

salt and pepper

Put the whole bell peppers on a baking sheet and place under a preheated broiler, turning frequently, for 15 minutes, until charred all over. Remove with tongs and place in a bowl. Cover with crumpled paper towels and set aside.

Meanwhile, bring a large pan of lightly salted water to a boil. Add the pasta, bring back to a boil, and cook for 8–10 minutes, until tender but still firm to the bite.

Combine the olive oil, lemon juice, pesto, and garlic in a bowl, whisking well to mix. Drain the pasta, add it to the pesto mixture while still hot, and toss well. Set aside.

When the bell peppers are cool enough to handle, peel off the skins, then cut open and remove the seeds. Chop the flesh coarsely and add to the pasta with the basil. Season to taste with salt and pepper and toss well. Serve at room temperature.

Rare Beef Pasta Salad

serves 4

1 lb/450 g sirloin or porterhouse steak in 1 piece

1 lb/450 g dried fusilli (pasta spirals)

4 tbsp olive oil

2 tbsp lime juice

2 tbsp Thai fish sauce

2 tsp honey

4 scallions, sliced

1 cucumber, peeled and cut into 1-inch/2.5-cm chunks

3 tomatoes, cut into wedges

3 tsp finely chopped fresh mint

salt and pepper

Season the steak with salt and pepper. Broil or pan-fry the steak for about 4 minutes on each side. Let stand for 5 minutes, then slice thinly across the grain.

Meanwhile, bring a large pan of lightly salted water to a boil over medium heat. Add the pasta and cook for 8–10 minutes, or until tender but still firm to the bite. Drain the pasta thoroughly, then refresh in cold water and drain again. Return the pasta to the pan and toss in the oil.

Mix the lime juice, fish sauce, and honey together in a small pan and cook over medium heat for about 2 minutes.

Add the scallions, cucumber, tomatoes, and chopped mint to the pan, then add the steak and mix well. Season with salt to taste.

Transfer the pasta to a large, warmed serving dish and top with the steak mixture. Serve just warm or let cool completely.

Spicy Sausage Pasta Salad

serves 4

$4\frac{1}{2}$ oz/125 g dried conchiglie (pasta shells)

2 tbsp olive oil

1 medium onion, chopped

2 garlic cloves, very finely chopped

1 small yellow bell pepper, seeded and cut into very thin sticks

6 oz/175 g spicy pork sausage, such as chorizo, pepperoni, or salami, skinned and sliced

2 tbsp red wine

1 tbsp red wine vinegar

4 oz/125 g mixed salad greens

salt

Bring a large pan of lightly salted water to a boil over medium heat. Add the pasta and cook for 8–10 minutes, or until tender but still firm to the bite. Drain and set aside.

Heat the oil in a pan over medium heat. Add the onion and cook until translucent, then stir in the garlic, yellow bell pepper, and sausage, and cook for 3–4 minutes, stirring once or twice.

Add the wine, vinegar, and reserved pasta to the pan, stir, and bring the mixture just to a boil over medium heat.

Arrange the salad greens on serving plates, spoon over the warm sausage and pasta mixture, and serve immediately.

Pasta Salad with Melon & Shrimp

serves 6

8 oz/225 g dried green fusilli (pasta spirals)

5 tbsp extra virgin olive oil

1 lb/450 g cooked shrimp

1 cantaloupe melon

1 honeydew melon

1 tbsp red wine vinegar

1 tsp whole grain mustard

pinch of superfine sugar

1 tbsp chopped fresh flat-leaf parsley

1 tbsp chopped fresh basil, plus extra sprigs to garnish

1 oak leaf lettuce, shredded

salt and pepper

Bring a large pan of salted water to a boil. Add the pasta, bring back to a boil, and cook for 8–10 minutes, or until tender but still firm to the bite. Drain, toss with 1 tablespoon of the olive oil, and let cool.

Meanwhile, peel and devein the shrimp, then place them in a large bowl. Halve both the melons and scoop out the seeds with a spoon. Using a melon baller or teaspoon, scoop out balls of the flesh and add them to the shrimp.

Whisk together the remaining olive oil, the vinegar, mustard, sugar, parsley, and basil in a small bowl. Season to taste with salt and pepper. Add the cooled pasta to the shrimp and melon mixture and toss lightly to mix, then pour in the dressing, and toss again. Cover with plastic wrap and chill in the refrigerator for 30 minutes.

Make a bed of shredded lettuce on a serving plate. Spoon the pasta salad on top, garnish with basil leaves, and serve.

Neapolitan Seafood Salad

serves 4

1 lb/450 g prepared squid, cut into strips

1 lb 10 oz/750 g cooked mussels

1 lb/450 g cooked baby clams in brine, drained

5/8 cup white wine

1½ cups olive oil

2 cups dried orecchiette

juice of 1 lemon

1 bunch chives, snipped

1 bunch fresh parsley, finely chopped

mixed salad greens

4 large tomatoes, quartered

salt and pepper

Put all of the seafood into a large bowl. Pour over the wine and half the olive oil, then set aside for 6 hours.

Put the seafood mixture into a pan and simmer over a low heat for 10 minutes. Set aside to cool.

Bring a large pan of lightly salted water to a boil. Add the pasta and 1 tbsp of the remaining olive oil and cook for 8–10 minutes, or until tender but still firm to the bite. Drain thoroughly and refresh in cold water.

Strain off about half of the cooking liquid from the seafood and discard the rest. Mix in the lemon juice, chives, parsley, and the remaining olive oil. Season to taste with salt and pepper. Drain the pasta and add to the seafood.

Shred the salad leaves and arrange them in the base of a salad bowl. Spoon the seafood salad into the bowl, top with the tomatoes, and serve.

Tuna & Fusilli Salad

serves 4

7 oz/200 g dried fusilli

1 red bell pepper, seeded and quartered

1 red onion, sliced

4 tomatoes, sliced

7 oz/200 g canned tuna in brine, drained and flaked

salt

for the dressing

6 tbsp basil-flavored oil or extra virgin olive oil

3 tbsp white wine vinegar

1 tbsp lime juice

1 tsp mustard

1 tsp honey

4 tbsp chopped fresh basil, plus extra sprigs to garnish

Bring a large pan of lightly salted water to a boil. Add the pasta, return to a boil, and cook for 8–10 minutes, or until tender but still firm to the bite.

Meanwhile, put the bell pepper quarters under a preheated hot broiler and cook for 10–12 minutes until the skins begin to blacken. Transfer to a plastic bag, seal, and set aside.

Remove the pasta from the heat, drain, and set aside to cool. Remove the bell pepper quarters from the bag and peel off the skins. Slice the bell pepper into strips.

To make the dressing, put all the dressing ingredients in a large bowl and stir together well. Add the pasta, bell pepper strips, onion, tomatoes, and tuna. Toss together gently, garnish with basil springs, and serve.

2

Meat & Poultry

Spaghetti Bolognese

serves 4

1 tbsp olive oil
1 onion, finely chopped
2 garlic cloves, chopped
1 carrot, chopped
1 celery stalk, chopped
1¾ oz/50 g pancetta or bacon, diced
12 oz/350 g lean ground beef
14 oz/400 g canned chopped tomatoes
2 tsp dried oregano
½ cup red wine
2 tbsp tomato paste
12 oz/350 g dried spaghetti
salt and pepper
chopped fresh flat-leaf parsley, to garnish

Heat the oil in a large skillet. Add the onion and cook for 3 minutes. Add the garlic, carrot, celery, and pancetta and cook for 3–4 minutes, or until just beginning to brown.

Add the beef and cook over high heat for an additional 3 minutes, or until the meat has browned. Stir in the tomatoes, oregano, and red wine and bring to a boil. Reduce the heat and simmer for about 45 minutes.

Stir in the tomato paste and season to taste with salt and pepper.

Cook the spaghetti in a pan of lightly salted boiling water for 8–10 minutes, or until tender but still firm to the bite. Drain thoroughly.

Transfer the spaghetti to a warmed serving dish and pour over the bolognese sauce. Toss to mix well, garnish with parsley, and serve hot.

Spaghetti with Meatballs

serves 6

1 potato, diced
14 oz/400 g ground steak
1 onion, finely chopped
1 egg
4 tbsp chopped fresh flat-leaf parsley
all-purpose flour, for dusting
5 tbsp olive oil
1¾ cups strained canned tomatoes
2 tbsp tomato paste
14 oz/400 g dried spaghetti
salt and pepper
fresh basil leaves, to garnish
shavings of fresh Parmesan cheese, to garnish

Place the potato in a small pan, add cold water to cover and a pinch of salt, and bring to a boil. Cook for 10–15 minutes until tender, then drain. Either mash thoroughly with a potato masher or fork or pass through a potato ricer.

Combine the potato, steak, onion, egg, and parsley in a bowl and season to taste with salt and pepper. Spread out the flour on a plate. With dampened hands, shape the meat mixture into walnut-size balls and roll in the flour. Shake off any excess.

Heat the olive oil in a heavy-bottom skillet, add the meatballs, and cook over medium heat, stirring and turning frequently, for 8–10 minutes, or until golden all over.

Add the strained tomatoes and tomato paste and cook for an additional 10 minutes, or until the sauce is reduced and thickened.

Meanwhile, bring a large pan of lightly salted water to a boil. Add the pasta, return to a boil, and cook for 8–10 minutes, or until tender but still firm to the bite.

Drain well and add to the meatball sauce, tossing well to coat. Transfer to a warmed serving dish, garnish with the basil leaves and Parmesan cheese, and serve immediately.

Spaghetti alla Carbonara

serves 4

1 lb/450 g dried spaghetti

1 tbsp olive oil

8 oz/225 g rindless pancetta or lean bacon, chopped

4 eggs

5 tbsp light cream

2 tbsp freshly grated Parmesan cheese

salt and pepper

Bring a large, heavy-bottom pan of lightly salted water to a boil. Add the pasta, return to a boil, and cook for 8–10 minutes, or until tender but still firm to the bite.

Meanwhile, heat the oil in a heavy-bottom skillet. Add the pancetta and cook over medium heat, stirring frequently, for 8–10 minutes.

Beat the eggs with the cream in a small bowl and season to taste with salt and pepper. Drain the pasta and return it to the pan. Turn in the contents of the skillet, then add the egg mixture and half the Parmesan cheese. Stir well, then transfer to a warmed serving dish. Serve immediately, sprinkled with the remaining cheese.

Fusilli with Bacon, Eggs & Mushrooms

serves 6

1 tbsp olive oil

4 strips lean bacon or pancetta

2 cups mushrooms, sliced

2 cups dried fusilli

2 eggs, beaten

4 oz/115 g Cheddar or mozzarella cheese, cubed

salt and pepper

chopped fresh flat-leaf parsley, to garnish

Heat the oil in a skillet over a medium heat. Add the bacon and cook until crisp. Remove with tongs, cut into small pieces and keep warm.

Cook the mushrooms in the pan with the bacon fat for 5–7 minutes, or until soft. Remove from the heat.

Cook the pasta in a pan of lightly salted boiling water for 8–10 minutes, or until tender but still firm to the bite.

Stir the mushrooms, beaten eggs, and the cheese cubes into the pasta. Season with pepper and toss until the eggs have coated the pasta and the cheese has melted.

Transfer to a warmed serving dish. Sprinkle with the bacon pieces and parsley and serve at once.

Pasta with Bacon & Tomatoes

serves 4

2 lb/900 g small, sweet tomatoes

6 slices rindless smoked bacon

4 tbsp butter

1 onion, chopped

1 garlic clove, crushed

4 fresh oregano sprigs, finely chopped

1 lb/450 g dried orecchiette (ear-shaped pasta)

salt and pepper

freshly grated Romano cheese, to serve

Blanch the tomatoes in boiling water. Drain, peel, and seed the tomatoes, then coarsely chop the flesh.

Using a sharp knife, chop the bacon into small dice. Melt the butter in a pan. Add the bacon and cook until it is golden.

Add the onion and garlic, and cook over medium heat for 5–7 minutes, until just softened.

Add the tomatoes and oregano to the pan, then season to taste with salt and pepper. Lower the heat and simmer for 10–12 minutes.

Bring a large pan of lightly salted water to a boil. Add the pasta and cook for 8–10 minutes, or until just tender but still firm to the bite. Drain the pasta and transfer to a warmed serving dish.

Spoon the bacon and tomato sauce over the pasta, toss to coat, and serve with the Romano cheese.

Linguine with Bacon & Olives

serves 4

3 tbsp olive oil

2 onions, thinly sliced

2 garlic cloves, finely chopped

6 oz/175 g rindless lean bacon, diced

8 oz/225 g mushrooms, sliced

5 canned anchovy fillets, drained

6 black olives, pitted and halved

1 lb/450 g dried linguine

1/4 cup freshly grated Parmesan cheese

salt and pepper

Heat the olive oil in a large skillet. Add the onions, garlic, and bacon, and cook over low heat, stirring occasionally, until the onions are softened. Stir in the mushrooms, anchovies, and olives, then season to taste with salt, if necessary, and pepper. Simmer for 5 minutes.

Meanwhile, bring a large, heavy-bottom pan of lightly salted water to a boil. Add the pasta, return to a boil, and cook for 8–10 minutes, or until tender but still firm to the bite.

Drain the pasta and transfer to a warmed serving dish. Spoon the sauce on top, toss lightly, and sprinkle with the Parmesan cheese. Serve immediately.

Farfalle with Gorgonzola & Ham

serves 4

1 cup crème fraîche or sour cream

8 oz/225 g cremini mushrooms, quartered

14 oz/400 g dried farfalle (pasta bows)

3 oz/85 g Gorgonzola cheese, crumbled

1 tbsp chopped fresh flat-leaf parsley, plus extra sprigs to garnish

1 cup cooked ham, diced

salt and pepper

Pour the crème fraîche into a pan, add the mushrooms, and season to taste with salt and pepper. Bring to just below a boil, then lower the heat, and simmer very gently, stirring occasionally, for 8–10 minutes, until the cream has thickened.

Meanwhile, bring a large pan of lightly salted water to a boil. Add the pasta, bring back to a boil, and cook for 8–10 minutes, until tender but still firm to the bite.

Remove the pan of mushrooms from the heat and stir in the Gorgonzola cheese until it has melted. Return the pan to very low heat and stir in the chopped parsley and ham.

Drain the pasta and add it to the sauce. Toss lightly, then divide among individual warmed dishes, garnish with the parsley sprigs, and serve.

Penne with Ham, Tomato & Chile

serves 4

1 tbsp olive oil

2 tbsp butter

1 onion, finely chopped

⅔ cup diced ham

2 garlic cloves, very finely chopped

1 red chile, seeded and finely chopped

1 lb 12 oz/800 g canned chopped tomatoes

1 lb/450 g dried penne (pasta quills)

2 tbsp chopped fresh flat-leaf parsley

6 tbsp freshly grated Parmesan cheese

salt and pepper

Put the olive oil and 1 tablespoon of the butter in a large skillet over medium–low heat. Add the onion and cook for 10 minutes, or until soft and golden. Add the ham and cook for an additional 5 minutes, or until lightly browned. Stir in the garlic, chile, and tomatoes. Season to taste with salt and pepper. Bring to a boil, then simmer over medium–low heat for 30–40 minutes, or until thickened.

Cook the pasta in a pan of lightly salted boiling water for 8–10 minutes, or until tender but still firm to the bite. Drain and transfer to a warmed serving dish.

Pour the sauce over the pasta. Add the parsley, Parmesan cheese, and the remaining butter. Toss well to mix and serve immediately.

Saffron Linguine

serves 4

12 oz/350 g dried linguine

pinch of saffron threads

2 tbsp water

5 oz/140 g ham, cut into strips

3/4 cup heavy cream

1/2 cup freshly grated Parmesan cheese

2 egg yolks

salt and pepper

Bring a large, heavy-bottom pan of lightly salted water to a boil. Add the pasta, return to a boil, and cook for 8–10 minutes, or until tender but still firm to the bite.

Meanwhile, place the saffron in a separate heavy-bottom pan and add the water. Bring to a boil, then remove from the heat and let stand for 5 minutes.

Stir the ham, cream, and Parmesan cheese into the saffron and return the pan to the heat. Season to taste with salt and pepper and heat through gently, stirring constantly, until simmering. Remove the pan from the heat and beat in the egg yolks. Drain the pasta and transfer to a large, warmed serving dish. Add the saffron sauce, toss well, and serve.

Penne with Sausage Sauce

serves 4–6

2 tbsp olive oil

1 red onion, coarsely chopped

2 garlic cloves, coarsely chopped

6 Italian sausages, skinned and the meat crumbled

½ tsp dried chile flakes

2 tbsp chopped fresh oregano

14 oz/400 g canned chopped tomatoes

12 oz/350 g dried penne

salt and pepper

2 tbsp chopped fresh flat-leaf parsley, to garnish

3 tbsp freshly grated Parmesan cheese, to serve

Heat the oil in a large pan, then add the onion and cook over medium heat, stirring frequently, for 6–8 minutes, or until starting to brown. Add the garlic and the crumbled sausages and cook for 8–10 minutes, breaking up the sausages with a wooden spoon.

Add the chile flakes and oregano and stir well. Pour in the tomatoes and bring to a boil, then reduce the heat and simmer, uncovered, for 4–5 minutes, or until reduced and thickened. Season to taste with salt and pepper.

Meanwhile, bring a large pan of salted water to a boil. Add the pasta and stir well, then return to a boil and cook for 8–10 minutes, or until tender but still firm to the bite. Drain well and return to the pan.

Pour the sauce into the pasta and stir well.

Transfer to warmed serving dishes, garnish with parsley, and serve immediately with Parmesan cheese.

Pepperoni Pasta

serves 4

3 tbsp olive oil

1 onion, chopped

1 red bell pepper, seeded and diced

1 orange bell pepper, seeded and diced

1 lb 12 oz/800 g canned chopped tomatoes

1 tbsp sun-dried tomato paste

1 tsp paprika

8 oz/225 g pepperoni sausage, sliced

2 tbsp chopped fresh flat-leaf parsley, plus extra to garnish

1 lb/450 g dried penne (pasta quills)

salt and pepper

Heat 2 tablespoons of the oil in a large, heavy-bottom skillet. Add the onion and cook over low heat, stirring occasionally, for 5 minutes, or until softened. Add the red and orange bell peppers, tomatoes and their can juices, sun-dried tomato paste, and paprika and bring to a boil.

Add the pepperoni and parsley and season to taste with salt and pepper. Stir well, bring to a boil, then reduce the heat and simmer for 10–15 minutes.

Meanwhile, bring a large, heavy-bottom pan of lightly salted water to a boil. Add the pasta, return to a boil, and cook for 8–10 minutes, or until tender but still firm to the bite. Drain well and transfer to a warmed serving dish. Add the remaining olive oil and toss. Add the sauce and toss again. Sprinkle with parsley and serve immediately.

Rigatoni with Chorizo & Mushrooms

serves 4

4 tbsp olive oil
1 red onion, chopped
1 garlic clove, chopped
1 celery stalk, sliced
14 oz/400 g dried rigatoni (pasta tubes)
10 oz/280 g chorizo sausage, sliced
8 oz/225 g cremini mushrooms, halved
1 tbsp chopped fresh cilantro
1 tbsp lime juice
salt and pepper

Heat the oil in a skillet. Add the onion, garlic, and celery and cook over low heat, stirring occasionally, for 5 minutes, until softened.

Meanwhile, bring a large pan of lightly salted water to a boil. Add the pasta, bring back to a boil, and cook for 8–10 minutes, or until tender but still firm to the bite.

While the pasta is cooking, add the chorizo to the skillet and cook, stirring occasionally, for 5 minutes, until evenly browned. Add the mushrooms and cook, stirring occasionally, for an additional 5 minutes. Stir in the cilantro and lime juice and season to taste with salt and pepper.

Drain the pasta and return it to the pan. Add the chorizo and mushroom mixture and toss lightly. Divide among warmed serving dishes and serve immediately.

Pasticcio

serves 4

1 tbsp olive oil
1 onion, chopped
2 garlic cloves, finely chopped
2 cups fresh ground lamb
2 tbsp tomato paste
2 tbsp all-purpose flour
1¼ cups chicken stock
1 tsp ground cinnamon
4 oz/115 g dried macaroni
2 beefsteak tomatoes, sliced
1¼ cups strained plain yogurt
2 eggs, lightly beaten
salt and pepper
salad leaves, to serve

Preheat the oven to 375°F/190°C. Heat the oil in a large, heavy-bottom skillet. Add the onion and garlic and cook over low heat, stirring occasionally, for 5 minutes, or until softened. Add the lamb and cook, breaking it up with a wooden spoon, until browned all over. Add the tomato paste and sprinkle in the flour. Cook, stirring, for 1 minute, then stir in the stock. Season to taste with salt and pepper and stir in the cinnamon. Bring to a boil, reduce the heat, cover, and cook for 25 minutes.

Meanwhile, bring a large, heavy-bottom pan of lightly salted water to a boil. Add the pasta, return to a boil, and cook for 8–10 minutes, or until tender but still firm to the bite.

Drain the pasta and stir into the lamb mixture. Spoon into a large ovenproof dish and arrange the tomato slices on top. Beat together the yogurt and eggs then spoon over the lamb mixture. Bake in the preheated oven for 1 hour. Serve immediately with salad greens.

Chicken with Creamy Penne

serves 2

7 oz/200 g dried penne
1 tbsp olive oil
2 skinless, boneless chicken breasts
4 tbsp dry white wine
heaping 1 cup frozen peas
5 tbsp heavy cream
salt
4–5 tbsp chopped fresh flat-leaf parsley, to garnish

Bring a large, heavy-bottom pan of lightly salted water to a boil. Add the pasta, return to a boil and cook for 8–10 minutes, or until tender but still firm to the bite.

Meanwhile, heat the oil in a skillet, add the chicken breasts, and cook over medium heat for about 4 minutes on each side.

Pour in the wine and cook over high heat until it has almost evaporated.

Drain the pasta. Add the peas, cream, and pasta to the chicken breasts in the skillet and stir well. Cover and simmer for 2 minutes. Serve immediately sprinkled with chopped parsley.

Spaghetti with Parsley Chicken

serves 4

1 tbsp olive oil

thinly pared rind of 1 lemon, cut into julienne strips

1 tsp finely chopped fresh ginger

1 tsp sugar

1 cup chicken stock

9 oz/250 g dried spaghetti

4 tbsp butter

8 oz/225 g skinless, boneless chicken breasts, diced

1 red onion, finely chopped

leaves from 2 bunches of fresh flat-leaf parsley

salt

Heat the oil in a heavy-bottom pan. Add the lemon rind and cook over low heat, stirring frequently, for 5 minutes. Stir in the ginger and sugar, season to taste with salt, and cook, stirring constantly, for an additional 2 minutes. Pour in the chicken stock, bring to a boil, then cook for 5 minutes, or until the liquid has reduced by half.

Meanwhile, bring a large, heavy-bottom pan of lightly salted water to a boil. Add the pasta, return to a boil, and cook for 8–10 minutes, or until tender but still firm to the bite.

Melt half the butter in a skillet. Add the chicken and onion and cook, stirring frequently, for 5 minutes, or until the chicken is lightly browned all over. Stir in the lemon and ginger mixture and cook for 1 minute. Stir in the parsley leaves and cook, stirring constantly, for an additional 3 minutes.

Drain the pasta and transfer to a warmed serving dish, then add the remaining butter and toss well. Add the chicken sauce, toss again, and serve.

Penne with Chicken & Feta

serves 4

2 tbsp olive oil

1 lb/450 g skinless, boneless chicken breasts, cut into thin strips

6 scallions, chopped

8 oz/225 g feta cheese, diced

4 tbsp snipped fresh chives

1 lb/450 g dried penne (pasta quills)

salt and pepper

Heat the oil in a heavy-bottom skillet. Add the chicken and cook over medium heat, stirring frequently, for 5–8 minutes, or until golden all over and cooked through. Add the scallions and cook for 2 minutes. Stir the feta cheese into the skillet with half the chives and season to taste with salt and pepper.

Meanwhile, bring a large, heavy-bottom pan of lightly salted water to a boil. Add the pasta, return to a boil, and cook for 8–10 minutes, or until tender but still firm to the bite. Drain well, then transfer to a warmed serving dish.

Spoon the chicken mixture onto the pasta, toss lightly, and serve immediately, garnished with the remaining chives.

Farfalle with Chicken & Broccoli

serves 4

4 tbsp olive oil

5 tbsp butter

3 garlic cloves, very finely chopped

1 lb/450 g boneless, skinless chicken breasts, diced

1/4 tsp dried chile flakes

1 lb/450 g small broccoli florets

10 1/2 oz/300 g dried farfalle (pasta bows)

6 oz/175 g bottled roasted red bell peppers, drained and diced

1 cup chicken stock

salt and pepper

Bring a large pan of lightly salted water to a boil. Meanwhile, heat the oil and butter in a large skillet over medium–low heat. Add the garlic and cook until just beginning to color.

Add the diced chicken, then raise the heat to medium and cook for 4–5 minutes, or until the chicken is no longer pink. Add the chile flakes and season to taste with salt and pepper. Remove from the heat.

Plunge the broccoli into the boiling water and cook for 2 minutes. Remove with a slotted spoon and set aside. Bring the water back to a boil. Add the pasta and cook for 8–10 minutes, or until tender but still firm to the bite. Drain and add to the chicken mixture in the pan. Add the broccoli and roasted bell peppers. Pour in the stock. Simmer briskly over medium–high heat, stirring frequently, until most of the liquid has been absorbed.

Transfer to warmed serving dishes and serve.

Italian Chicken Spirals

serves 4

4 skinless, boneless chicken breasts

1 cup fresh basil leaves

1 tbsp hazelnuts

1 garlic clove, crushed

9 oz/250 g dried whole wheat fusilli

2 sun-dried tomatoes or fresh tomatoes

1 tbsp lemon juice

1 tbsp olive oil

1 tbsp capers

½ cup pitted black olives

salt and pepper

Beat the chicken breasts with a rolling pin to flatten evenly.

Place the basil and hazelnuts in a food processor and process until finely chopped. Mix with the garlic and salt and pepper to taste.

Spread the basil mixture over the chicken breasts and roll up from one short end to enclose the filling. Wrap the chicken rolls tightly in foil so that they hold their shape, then seal the ends well.

Bring a pan of lightly salted water to a boil and cook the pasta for 8–10 minutes, or until tender but still firm to the bite. Meanwhile, place the chicken parcels in a steamer or colander set over the pan, cover tightly, and steam for 10 minutes.

Using a sharp knife, dice the tomatoes.

Drain the pasta and return to the pan with the lemon juice, oil, tomatoes, capers, and olives. Warm through.

Pierce the chicken with a skewer to make sure that the juices run clear. Slice the chicken, arrange over the pasta in a warm serving dish and serve.

3

Fish & Seafood

Spaghetti alla Puttanesca

serves 4

3 tbsp olive oil

2 garlic cloves, finely chopped

10 canned anchovy fillets, drained and chopped

1 cup black olives, pitted and chopped

1 tbsp capers, drained and rinsed

1 lb/450 g plum tomatoes, peeled, seeded, and chopped

pinch of cayenne pepper

14 oz/400 g dried spaghetti

salt

2 tbsp chopped fresh flat-leaf parsley, to garnish (optional)

Heat the oil in a heavy-bottom skillet. Add the garlic and cook over low heat, stirring frequently, for 2 minutes. Add the anchovies and mash them to a pulp with a fork. Add the olives, capers, and tomatoes, and season to taste with cayenne pepper. Cover and simmer for 25 minutes.

Meanwhile, bring a large, heavy-bottom pan of lightly salted water to a boil. Add the pasta, return to a boil, and cook for 8–10 minutes, or until tender but still firm to the bite. Drain well and transfer to a warmed serving dish.

Spoon the anchovy sauce into the dish and toss the pasta, using 2 large forks. Garnish with the chopped parsley, if using, and serve immediately.

Penne with Sicilian Sauce

serves 4

½ cup golden raisins

1 lb/450 g tomatoes, halved

¼ cup pine nuts

1¾ oz/50 g canned anchovies, drained and halved lengthwise

2 tbsp tomato paste

12 oz/350 g dried penne (pasta quills)

Soak the golden raisins in a bowl of warm water for about 20 minutes. Drain them thoroughly.

Preheat the broiler, then cook the tomatoes under the hot broiler for 10 minutes. Let cool slightly, then once cool enough to handle, peel off the skin and dice the flesh. Place the pine nuts on a cookie sheet and lightly toast under the broiler for 2–3 minutes, or until golden brown.

Place the tomatoes, pine nuts, and golden raisins in a small pan and heat gently. Add the anchovies and tomato paste, and cook the sauce over low heat for an additional 2–3 minutes, or until hot.

Meanwhile, bring a large, heavy-bottom pan of lightly salted water to a boil. Add the pasta, return to a boil, and cook for 8–10 minutes, or until tender but still firm to the bite. Drain thoroughly, then transfer the pasta to a serving dish and serve with the Sicilian sauce.

Fettuccine with Spinach & Anchovies

serves 4

2 lb/900 g fresh baby spinach leaves

14 oz/400 g dried fettuccine

5 tbsp olive oil

3 tbsp pine nuts

3 garlic cloves, crushed

8 canned anchovy fillets, drained and chopped

salt

Trim off any tough spinach stalks. Rinse the spinach leaves under cold running water and place them in a large pan with only the water that is clinging to them after washing. Cover and cook over high heat, shaking the pan from time to time, until the spinach has wilted, but retains its color. Drain well, set aside, and keep warm.

Bring a large, heavy-bottom pan of lightly salted water to a boil. Add the fettuccine, return to a boil, and cook for 8–10 minutes, or until tender but still firm to the bite.

Heat 4 tablespoons of the oil in a separate pan. Add the pine nuts and cook until golden. Remove the pine nuts from the pan and set aside until needed.

Add the garlic to the pan and cook until golden. Add the anchovies and stir in the spinach. Cook, stirring, for 2–3 minutes, until heated through. Return the pine nuts to the pan.

Drain the fettuccine, toss in the remaining oil, and transfer to a warmed serving dish. Spoon the anchovy and spinach sauce over the fettuccine, toss lightly, and serve immediately.

Spaghetti with Tuna & Parsley

serves 6

1 lb 2 oz/500 g dried spaghetti

2 tbsp butter

7 oz/200 g canned tuna, drained

2 oz/55 g canned anchovies, drained

1 cup olive oil

1 cup coarsely chopped fresh flat-leaf parsley, plus extra to garnish

2/3 cup sour cream or yogurt

salt and pepper

Bring a large, heavy-bottom pan of lightly salted water to a boil. Add the spaghetti, return to a boil, and cook for 8–10 minutes, or until tender but still firm to the bite. Drain the spaghetti in a colander and return to the pan. Add the butter, toss thoroughly to coat, and keep warm until needed.

Flake the tuna into smaller pieces using 2 forks. Place the tuna in a food processor or blender with the anchovies, oil, and parsley and process until the sauce is smooth. Pour in the sour cream and process for a few seconds to blend. Taste the sauce and season with salt and pepper, if necessary.

Shake the pan of spaghetti over medium heat for a few minutes, or until it is thoroughly warmed through.

Pour the sauce over the spaghetti and toss quickly, using 2 forks. Garnish with parsley and serve immediately.

Spaghettini with Quick Tuna Sauce

serves 4

3 tbsp olive oil

4 tomatoes, peeled, seeded, and coarsely chopped

4 oz/115 g mushrooms, sliced

1 tbsp shredded fresh basil

14 oz/400 g canned tuna, drained

1/3 cup fish or chicken stock

1 garlic clove, finely chopped

2 tsp chopped fresh marjoram

12 oz/350 g dried spaghettini

salt and pepper

1 cup freshly grated Parmesan cheese, to serve

Heat the oil in a large skillet. Add the tomatoes and cook over low heat, stirring occasionally, for 15 minutes, or until pulpy. Add the mushrooms and cook, stirring occasionally, for an additional 10 minutes. Stir in the basil, tuna, stock, garlic, and marjoram, and season to taste with salt and pepper. Cook over low heat for 5 minutes, or until heated through.

Meanwhile, bring a large, heavy-bottom pan of lightly salted water to a boil. Add the pasta, return to a boil, and cook for 8–10 minutes, or until tender but still firm to the bite.

Drain the pasta well, transfer to a warmed serving dish, and spoon on the tuna mixture. Serve with grated Parmesan cheese.

Baked Tuna & Ricotta Rigatoni

serves 4

butter, for greasing

1 lb/450 g dried rigatoni (pasta tubes)

7 oz/200 g canned flaked tuna, drained

1 cup ricotta cheese

½ cup heavy cream

2 cups freshly grated Parmesan cheese

4 oz/115 g sun-dried tomatoes, drained and sliced

salt and pepper

Preheat the oven to 400°F/200°C. Lightly grease a large ovenproof dish with butter. Bring a large, heavy-bottom pan of lightly salted water to a boil. Add the rigatoni, return to a boil, and cook for 8–10 minutes, or until tender but still firm to the bite. Drain the pasta and let stand until cool enough to handle.

Meanwhile, mix the tuna and ricotta cheese together in a bowl to form a soft paste. Spoon the mixture into a pastry bag and use to fill the rigatoni. Arrange the filled pasta tubes side by side in the prepared dish.

To make the sauce, mix the cream and Parmesan cheese together in a bowl and season to taste with salt and pepper. Spoon the sauce over the rigatoni and top with the sun-dried tomatoes, arranged in a crisscross pattern. Bake in the preheated oven for 20 minutes. Serve hot straight from the dish.

Tagliatelle with Smoked Salmon & Arugula

serves 4

12 oz/350 g dried tagliatelle

2 tbsp olive oil

1 garlic clove, finely chopped

4 oz/115 g smoked salmon, cut into thin strips

1¼ cups arugula

salt and pepper

Bring a large heavy-bottom pan of lightly salted water to a boil. Add the pasta, return to a boil, and cook for 8–10 minutes, or until tender but still firm to the bite.

Just before the end of the cooking time, heat the olive oil in a heavy-bottom skillet. Add the garlic and cook over low heat, stirring constantly, for 1 minute. Do not let the garlic brown or it will taste bitter.

Add the salmon and arugula. Season to taste with pepper and cook, stirring constantly, for 1 minute. Remove the skillet from the heat.

Drain the pasta and transfer to a large, warmed serving dish. Add the smoked salmon and arugula mixture, toss lightly, and serve immediately.

Conchiglie with Smoked Salmon & Sour Cream

serves 4

1 lb/450 g dried conchiglie (pasta shells)

1¼ cups sour cream

2 tsp whole grain mustard

4 large scallions, sliced finely

8 oz/225 g smoked salmon, cut into bite-size pieces

finely grated rind of ½ lemon

salt and pepper

2 tbsp snipped fresh chives, to garnish

Bring a large, heavy-based saucepan of lightly salted water to a boil. Add the pasta, return to a boil and cook for 8–10 minutes, or until tender but still firm to the bite. Drain and return to the pan.

Add the sour cream, mustard, scallions, smoked salmon, and lemon rind to the pasta. Stir over a low heat until heated through. Season to taste with pepper.

Transfer to a warmed serving dish and garnish with the chives. Serve warm or at room temperature.

Fusilli with Monkfish & Broccoli

serves 4

4 oz/115 g head of broccoli, separated into florets

3 tbsp olive oil

12 oz/350 g monkfish fillet, skinned and cut into bite-size pieces

2 garlic cloves, crushed

½ cup dry white wine

1 cup heavy cream

14 oz/400 g dried fusilli (pasta spirals)

3 oz/85 g Gorgonzola cheese, diced

salt and pepper

Separate the broccoli florets into tiny sprigs. Bring a pan of lightly salted water to a boil, add the broccoli, and cook for 2 minutes. Drain and refresh under cold running water.

Heat the oil in a large heavy-bottom skillet. Add the monkfish and garlic and season to taste with salt and pepper. Cook, stirring frequently, for 5 minutes, or until the fish is opaque. Pour in the white wine and cream and cook, stirring occasionally, for 5 minutes, or until the fish is cooked through and the sauce has thickened. Stir in the broccoli.

Meanwhile, bring a large, heavy-bottom pan of lightly salted water to a boil. Add the pasta, return to a boil, and cook for 8–10 minutes, or until tender but still firm to the bite. Drain and turn the pasta into the pan with the fish, add the cheese, and toss lightly. Serve immediately.

Sea Bass with Olive Sauce

serves 4

1 lb/450 g dried macaroni

1 tbsp olive oil

8 x 4 oz/115 g sea bass medallions

for the sauce

2 tbsp butter

4 shallots, chopped

2 tbsp capers

1½ cups chopped, pitted green olives

4 tbsp balsamic vinegar

1¼ cups fish stock

1¼ cups heavy cream

juice of 1 lemon

salt and pepper

shredded leek, to garnish

shredded carrot, to garnish

To make the sauce, melt the butter in a skillet. Add the shallots and cook over a low heat for 4 minutes. Add the capers and olives and cook for a further 3 minutes.

Stir in the balsamic vinegar and fish stock. Bring to a boil and reduce by half. Add the cream, stirring, and reduce again by half. Season to taste with salt and pepper and stir in the lemon juice. Remove the pan from the heat; set aside and keep warm.

Bring a large pan of lightly salted water to the boil. Add the pasta and olive oil and cook for 8–10 minutes, or until tender but still firm to the bite.

Meanwhile, lightly broil the sea bass medallions for 3–4 minutes on each side, until cooked through, but still moist and delicate.

Drain the pasta thoroughly and transfer to warmed serving dishes. Top the pasta with the fish medallions and pour the olive sauce over. Garnish with shredded leek and carrot and serve immediately.

Tagliatelle with Creamy Shrimp

serves 4

- 3 tbsp olive oil
- 3 tbsp butter
- 4 garlic cloves, very finely chopped
- 2 tbsp finely diced red bell pepper
- 2 tbsp tomato paste
- ½ cup dry white wine
- 1 lb/450 g dried tagliatelle
- 12 oz/350 g raw shrimp, peeled, cut into ½-inch/1-cm pieces
- ½ cup heavy cream
- salt and pepper
- 3 tbsp chopped fresh flat-leaf parsley, to garnish

Heat the oil and butter in a pan over medium–low heat. Add the garlic and red bell pepper. Cook for a few seconds, or until the garlic is just beginning to color. Stir in the tomato paste and wine. Cook for 10 minutes, stirring.

Meawhile, bring a large saucepan of lightly salted water to a boil. Add the pasta, bring back to a boil, and cook for 8–10 minutes, or until tender but still firm to the bite. Drain and return to the pan.

Add the shrimp to the sauce and raise the heat to medium–high. Cook for 2 minutes, stirring, until the shrimp turn pink. Reduce the heat and stir in the cream. Cook for 1 minute, stirring constantly, until thickened. Season to taste with salt and pepper.

Transfer the pasta to a warmed serving dish. Pour the sauce over the pasta. Sprinkle with the parsley. Toss well to mix and serve at once.

Fusilli with Shrimp & Peas

serves 4

- pinch of saffron threads
- 1 cup dry white wine
- 3 tbsp olive oil
- 2 tbsp unsalted butter
- 1 shallot, chopped
- 2 cups peas
- 12 oz/350 g cooked peeled shrimp
- 12 oz/350 g dried fusilli
- salt and pepper
- 2 tbsp chopped fresh dill, to garnish

Place the saffron in a small bowl, add the wine, and let soak. Heat the olive oil and butter in a large heavy-bottom skillet. Add the shallot and cook over low heat, stirring occasionally, for 5 minutes, or until softened. Add the peas and shrimp and cook, stirring occasionally, for 2–3 minutes.

Bring a large heavy-bottom pan of lightly salted water to a boil. Add the pasta, return to a boil, and cook for 8–10 minutes, or until tender but still firm to the bite.

Meanwhile, stir the saffron and wine mixture into the skillet. Increase the heat and cook until the liquid is reduced by about half. Season to taste with salt and pepper. Drain the pasta and add to the skillet. Cook for 1–2 minutes, or until it is well coated with the sauce. Transfer to a warmed serving dish, sprinkle with dill, and serve.

Linguine with Shrimp & Scallops

serves 6

1 lb/450 g raw shrimp
2 tbsp butter
2 shallots, finely chopped
1 cup dry white vermouth
1½ cups water
1 lb/450 g dried linguine
2 tbsp olive oil
1 lb/450 g prepared scallops
2 tbsp chopped fresh chives
salt and pepper

Shell and devein the shrimp, reserving the shells. Melt the butter in a heavy-bottom skillet. Add the shallots and cook over low heat, stirring occasionally, for 5 minutes, or until softened. Add the shrimp shells and cook, stirring constantly, for 1 minute. Pour in the vermouth and cook, stirring, for 1 minute. Add the water, bring to a boil, then reduce the heat and let simmer for 10 minutes, or until the liquid has reduced by half. Remove the skillet from the heat.

Bring a large heavy-bottom pan of lightly salted water to a boil. Add the pasta, return to a boil, and cook for 8–10 minutes, or until tender but still firm to the bite.

Meanwhile, heat the oil in a separate heavy-bottom skillet. Add the scallops and shrimp and cook, stirring frequently, for 2 minutes, or until the scallops are opaque and the shrimp have changed color. Strain the shrimp-shell stock into the skillet. Drain the pasta and add to the skillet with the chives and season to taste with salt and pepper. Toss well over low heat for 1 minute, then serve.

Pappardelle with Scallops & Porcini Mushrooms

serves 4

1⅓ cups dried porcini mushrooms

2 cups hot water

3 tbsp olive oil

3 tbsp butter

1½ cups prepared scallops, sliced

2 garlic cloves, very finely chopped

2 tbsp lemon juice

1 cup heavy cream

12 oz/350 g dried pappardelle

salt and pepper

2 tbsp chopped fresh flat-leaf parsley, to garnish

Put the porcini mushrooms and hot water in a bowl. Let soak for 20 minutes. Strain the mushrooms, reserving the soaking water, and chop coarsely. Strain the liquid through a cheesecloth-lined fine-mesh strainer into a bowl.

Heat the oil and butter in a large skillet over medium heat. Add the scallops and cook for 2 minutes, or until just golden. Add the garlic and mushrooms, then cook for another minute.

Stir in the lemon juice, cream, and ½ cup of the strained mushroom water. Bring to a boil, then simmer over medium heat for 2–3 minutes, stirring constantly, until the liquid is reduced by half. Season to taste with salt and pepper. Remove from the heat.

Meanwhile, bring a large saucepan of lightly salted water to a boil. Add the pasta, bring back to a boil, and cook for 8–10 minutes, or until tender but still firm to the bite. Drain and transfer to a warmed serving dish. Briefly reheat the sauce and pour over the pasta. Sprinkle with the parsley and toss well to mix. Serve immediately.

Macaroni with Scallops & Pine Nuts

serves 4

14 oz/400 g dried long macaroni

4 tbsp olive oil

1 garlic clove, finely chopped

1/4 cup pine nuts

8 large prepared scallops, sliced

salt and pepper

2 tbsp fresh basil leaves, shredded, to garnish

Bring a large, heavy-bottom saucepan of lightly salted water to a boil. Add the pasta, return to a boil and cook for 8–10 minutes, or until tender but still firm to the bite.

About 5 minutes before the pasta is ready, heat the oil in a skillet. Add the garlic and cook for 1–2 minutes until softened but not browned. Add the pine nuts and cook until browned. Stir in the scallops and cook until just opaque. Season to taste with salt and pepper.

When the pasta is cooked, drain and return to the saucepan. Add the contents of the skillet to the pasta and toss together. Serve garnished with the shredded basil leaves.

Spaghetti Con Vongole

serves 4

2 lb 4 oz/1 kg live clams, scrubbed

¾ cup water

¾ cup dry white wine

12 oz/350 g dried spaghetti

5 tbsp olive oil

2 garlic cloves, finely chopped

4 tbsp chopped fresh flat-leaf parsley

salt and pepper

Discard any clams with broken shells or any that refuse to close when tapped. Place the clams in a large, heavy-bottom pan. Add the water and wine, then cover and cook over high heat, shaking the pan occasionally, for 5 minutes, or until the shells have opened. Remove the clams with a slotted spoon and strain the liquid through a cheesecloth-lined fine-mesh strainer into a small pan. Bring to a boil and cook until reduced by about half. Discard any clams that remain closed and remove the remainder from their shells.

Bring a large, heavy-bottom pan of lightly salted water to a boil. Add the pasta, return to a boil, and cook for 8–10 minutes, or until tender but still firm to the bite.

Meanwhile, heat the oil in a large, heavy-bottom skillet. Add the garlic and cook, stirring frequently, for 2 minutes. Add the parsley and the reduced cooking liquid and simmer gently. Drain the pasta and add it to the skillet with the clams. Season to taste with salt and pepper and cook, stirring constantly, for 4 minutes, or until the pasta is coated and the clams have heated through. Transfer to a warmed serving dish and serve immediately.

Spaghetti with Crab

serves 4

- 1 dressed crab, about 1 lb/ 450 g including the shell
- 12 oz/350 g dried spaghetti
- 6 tbsp extra virgin olive oil
- 1 red chile, seeded and finely chopped
- 2 garlic cloves, finely chopped
- 3 tbsp chopped fresh parsley
- 2 tbsp lemon juice
- 1 tsp finely grated lemon rind
- salt and pepper
- lemon wedges, to garnish

Using a knife, scoop the meat from the crab shell into a bowl. Mix the white and brown meat lightly together and set aside.

Bring a large pan of lightly salted water to a boil over medium heat. Add the pasta and cook for about 8–10 minutes, or until tender but still firm to the bite. Drain thoroughly and return to the pan.

Meanwhile, heat 2 tablespoons of the oil in a skillet over low heat. Add the chile and garlic and cook for 30 seconds, then add the crabmeat, parsley, lemon juice, and lemon rind. Cook for an additional minute, or until the crabmeat is just heated through.

Add the crab mixture to the pasta with the remaining oil and season to taste with salt and pepper. Toss together thoroughly, then transfer to a warmed serving dish. Garnish with a few lemon wedges and serve immediately.

Penne with Squid & Tomatoes

serves 4

8 oz/225 g dried penne (pasta quills)

12 oz/350 g prepared squid

6 tbsp olive oil

2 onions, sliced

1 cup fish stock or chicken stock

2/3 cup full-bodied red wine

14 oz/400 g canned chopped tomatoes

2 tbsp tomato paste

1 tbsp chopped fresh marjoram

1 bay leaf

salt and pepper

2 tbsp chopped fresh flat-leaf parsley, to garnish

Bring a large, heavy-bottom pan of lightly salted water to a boil. Add the pasta, return to a boil, and cook for 3 minutes, then drain and set aside until ready to use. With a sharp knife, cut the squid into strips.

Heat the olive oil in a large saucepan. Add the onions and cook over low heat, stirring occasionally, for 5 minutes, or until softened. Add the squid and stock, bring to a boil, and simmer for 3 minutes. Stir in the wine, chopped tomatoes and their can juices, tomato paste, marjoram, and bay leaf. Season to taste with salt and pepper. Bring to a boil and cook for 5 minutes, or until slightly reduced.

Add the pasta, return to a boil, and simmer for 8–10 minutes, or until tender but still firm to the bite. Remove and discard the bay leaf. Transfer to a warmed serving dish, sprinkle with the parsley, and serve immediately.

4

Vegetarian

Spaghetti with Tomato & Basil

serves 4

- 5 tbsp extra virgin olive oil
- 1 onion, finely chopped
- 1 lb 12 oz/800 g canned chopped tomatoes
- 4 garlic cloves, cut into quarters
- 1 lb/450 g dried spaghetti
- large handful fresh basil leaves, shredded
- salt and pepper
- shavings of fresh Parmesan cheese, to serve

Heat the oil in a large pan over medium heat. Add the onion and cook gently for 5 minutes, until soft. Add the tomatoes and garlic. Bring to a boil, then simmer over medium–low heat for 25–30 minutes, or until the oil separates from the tomato. Season to taste with salt and pepper.

Bring a large, heavy-bottom saucepan of lightly salted water to a boil. Add the pasta, bring back to a boil, and cook for 8–10 minutes, or until tender but still firm to the bite. Drain and transfer to a warmed serving dish.

Pour the sauce over the pasta. Add the basil and toss well to mix. Serve with Parmesan cheese.

Tagliatelle with Pesto

serves 4

1 lb/450 g dried tagliatelle

salt

fresh basil sprigs, to garnish

for the pesto

2 garlic cloves

¼ cup pine nuts

4 oz/115 g fresh basil leaves

½ cup olive oil

½ cup freshly grated Parmesan cheese

salt

To make the pesto, put the garlic, pine nuts, and a large pinch of salt into a food processor or blender and process briefly. Add the basil leaves and process to a paste. With the motor still running, gradually add the oil. Scrape into a bowl and beat in the Parmesan cheese. Season to taste with salt.

Bring a large pan of lightly salted water to a boil. Add the pasta, return to a boil, and cook for 8–10 minutes, or until tender but still firm to the bite. Drain the pasta well, return to the pan, and toss with half the pesto, then divide among warmed serving dishes and top with the remaining pesto. Garnish with basil and serve immediately.

Spaghetti Olio e Aglio

serves 4

1 lb/450 g dried spaghetti

½ cup extra virgin olive oil

3 garlic cloves, finely chopped

3 tbsp chopped fresh flat-leaf parsley

salt and pepper

Bring a large, heavy-bottom pan of lightly salted water to a boil. Add the pasta, return to a boil, and cook for 8–10 minutes, or until tender but still firm to the bite.

Meanwhile, heat the oil in a heavy-bottom skillet. Add the garlic and a pinch of salt and cook over low heat, stirring constantly, for 3–4 minutes, or until golden. Do not let the garlic brown or it will taste bitter. Remove the skillet from the heat.

Drain the pasta and transfer to a warmed serving dish. Pour in the garlic-flavored olive oil, then add the chopped parsley and season to taste with salt and pepper. Toss well and serve immediately.

Fettuccine with Garlic, Tomatoes & Olives

serves 4

4 plum tomatoes, peeled, seeded, and chopped

4 garlic cloves, finely chopped

8 black olives, pitted and finely chopped

1 red chile, seeded and finely chopped

2 tbsp chopped fresh flat-leaf parsley

2 tbsp extra virgin olive oil

1 tbsp lemon juice

10 oz/280 g dried fettuccine

salt and pepper

Place the tomatoes in a large, nonmetallic strainer set over a bowl. Cover and set aside in the refrigerator for 30 minutes.

Combine the garlic, olives, chile, parsley, oil, and lemon juice in a separate bowl. Season to taste with salt and pepper. Cover and set aside in the refrigerator until required.

Add the tomatoes to the garlic mixture, discarding the drained juice.

Bring a large pan of lightly salted water to a boil. Add the fettuccine, return to a boil, and cook for 8–10 minutes, or until tender but still firm to the bite. Drain, then tip into a warmed serving bowl. Add the garlic and tomato mixture and toss well. Serve immediately.

Creamy Pappardelle & Broccoli

serves 4

4 tbsp butter

1 large onion, finely chopped

1 lb/450 g dried pappardelle

1 lb/450 g head of broccoli, broken into florets

½ cup vegetable stock

1 tbsp all-purpose flour

½ cup light cream

½ cup freshly grated mozzarella cheese

freshly grated nutmeg

salt and white pepper

fresh apple slices, to garnish

Melt 2 tablespoons of the butter in a large pan over medium heat. Add the onion and cook for 4 minutes.

Add the pasta and broccoli to the pan and cook, stirring constantly, for 2 minutes. Add the stock, bring back to a boil, and simmer for 8–10 minutes. Season well with salt and white pepper.

Meanwhile, melt the remaining butter in a pan over medium heat. Sprinkle over the flour and cook, stirring constantly, for 2 minutes. Gradually stir in the cream and bring to a simmer, but do not boil. Add the mozzarella cheese and season to taste with salt and a little freshly grated nutmeg.

Drain the pasta and broccoli mixture and return to the pan. Pour over the cheese sauce and cook, stirring occasionally, for about 2 minutes. Transfer the pasta and broccoli mixture to warmed serving dishes and garnish with a few slices of apple. Serve.

Penne with Asparagus & Gorgonzola

serves 4

1 lb/450 g asparagus tips

olive oil

8 oz/225 g Gorgonzola cheese, crumbled

¾ cup heavy cream

3 cups dried penne

salt and pepper

Preheat the oven to 450°F/230°C. Place the asparagus tips in a single layer in a shallow ovenproof dish. Sprinkle with a little olive oil. Season to taste with salt and pepper. Turn to coat in the oil and seasoning.

Roast in the preheated oven for 10–12 minutes, or until slightly browned and just tender. Set aside and keep warm.

Combine the crumbled cheese with the cream in a bowl. Season to taste with salt and pepper.

Bring a large, heavy-bottom saucepan of lightly salted water to a boil. Add the pasta, return to a boil and cook for 8–10 minutes, or until tender but still firm to the bite. Drain and transfer to a warmed serving dish.

Immediately add the asparagus and the cheese mixture to the pasta. Toss well until the cheese has melted and the pasta is coated with the sauce. Serve immediately.

Fusilli with Ricotta, Mint & Garlic

serves 4

10½ oz/300 g dried fusilli

½ cup ricotta cheese

1–2 roasted garlic cloves from a jar, finely chopped

⅔ cup heavy cream

1 tbsp chopped fresh mint, plus extra sprigs to garnish

salt and pepper

Bring a large, heavy-bottom saucepan of lightly salted water to a boil. Add the pasta, return to a boil and cook for 8–10 minutes, or until tender but still firm to the bite.

Beat the ricotta, garlic, cream, and chopped mint together in a bowl until smooth.

Drain the cooked pasta then tip back into the pan. Pour in the cheese mixture and toss together.

Season to taste with pepper and serve immediately, garnished with the mint sprigs.

Rigatoni with Bell Peppers & Goat Cheese

serves 4

2 tbsp olive oil

1 tbsp butter

1 small onion, finely chopped

4 bell peppers, yellow and red, seeded and cut into ¾-inch/2-cm squares

3 garlic cloves, thinly sliced

1 lb/450 g dried rigatoni (pasta tubes)

4½ oz/125 g goat cheese, crumbled

15 fresh basil leaves, shredded

10 black olives, pitted and sliced

salt and pepper

Heat the oil and butter in a large skillet over medium heat. Add the onion and cook until soft. Raise the heat to medium–high and add the bell peppers and garlic. Cook for 12–15 minutes, stirring, until the peppers are tender but not mushy. Season to taste with salt and pepper. Remove from the heat.

Bring a large saucepan of lightly salted water to a boil. Add the pasta, bring back to a boil, and cook for 8–10 minutes, or until tender but still firm to the bite. Drain and transfer to a warmed serving dish. Add the goat cheese and toss to mix.

Briefly reheat the onion and pepper mixture. Add the basil and olives. Pour over the pasta and toss well to mix. Serve immediately.

Tagliatelle with Wild Mushrooms & Mascarpone

serves 4

1 lb/450 g dried linguine

2 oz/55 g butter

1 garlic clove, crushed

8 oz/225 g mixed wild mushrooms, sliced

generous 1 cup mascarpone cheese

2 tbsp milk

1 tsp chopped fresh sage

salt and pepper

freshly grated Parmesan cheese, to serve

Bring a large, heavy-bottom saucepan of lightly salted water to a boil. Add the pasta, return to a boil and cook for 8–10 minutes, or until tender but still firm to the bite.

Meanwhile, melt the butter in a separate large pan. Add the garlic and mushrooms and cook for 3–4 minutes.

Reduce the heat and stir in the mascarpone cheese, milk, and sage. Season to taste with salt and pepper.

Drain the pasta thoroughly and add to the mushroom sauce. Toss until the pasta is well coated with the sauce. Transfer to warmed dishes and serve immediately with Parmesan cheese.

Spaghetti alla Norma

serves 4

¾ cup olive oil

1 lb 2 oz/500 g plum tomatoes, peeled and chopped

1 garlic clove, chopped

12 oz/350 g eggplant, diced

14 oz/400 g dried spaghetti

½ bunch fresh basil, torn

1⅓ cups freshly grated Romano cheese

salt and pepper

Heat 4 tablespoons of the oil in a large pan. Add the tomatoes and garlic, season to taste with salt and pepper, cover, and cook over low heat, stirring occasionally, for 25 minutes.

Meanwhile, heat the remaining oil in a heavy skillet. Add the eggplant and cook, stirring occasionally, for 5 minutes, until evenly golden brown. Remove with a slotted spoon and drain on paper towels.

Bring a large pan of lightly salted water to a boil. Add the pasta, bring back to a boil, and cook for 8–10 minutes, until tender but still firm to the bite.

Meanwhile, stir the drained eggplant into the pan of tomatoes. Taste and adjust the seasoning, if necessary.

Drain the pasta and place in a warmed serving dish. Add the tomato and eggplant mixture, basil, and half the Romano cheese. Toss well, sprinkle with the remaining cheese, and serve immediately.

Fusilli with Zucchini & Lemon

serves 4

- 6 tbsp olive oil
- 1 small onion, very thinly sliced
- 2 garlic cloves, very finely chopped
- 2 tbsp chopped fresh rosemary
- 1 tbsp chopped fresh flat-leaf parsley
- 1 lb/450 g small zucchini, cut into 1½-inch/4-cm lengths
- finely grated rind of 1 lemon
- 1 lb/450 g dried fusilli (pasta spirals)
- salt and pepper
- freshly grated Parmesan cheese, to serve

Heat the oil in a large skillet over medium–low heat. Add the onion and cook gently, stirring occasionally, for about 10 minutes, or until golden.

Raise the heat to medium–high. Add the garlic, rosemary, and parsley. Cook for a few seconds, stirring.

Add the zucchini and lemon rind. Cook for 5–7 minutes, stirring occasionally, until the zucchini are just tender. Season to taste with salt and pepper. Remove from the heat.

Bring a large saucepan of lightly salted water to a boil. Add the pasta, bring back to a boil, and cook for 8–10 minutes, or until tender but still firm to the bite. Drain and transfer to a warmed serving dish.

Briefly reheat the zucchini sauce. Pour over the pasta and toss well to mix. Sprinkle with the Parmesan cheese and serve immediately.

Fusili with Sun-Dried Tomatoes

serves 4

3 oz/85 g sun-dried tomatoes (not in oil)

3 cups boiling water

2 tbsp olive oil

1 onion, finely chopped

2 large garlic cloves, finely sliced

2 tbsp chopped fresh flat-leaf parsley

2 tsp chopped fresh oregano

1 tsp chopped fresh rosemary

12 oz/350 g dried fusilli (pasta spirals)

10 fresh basil leaves, shredded

salt and pepper

3 tbsp freshly grated Parmesan cheese, to serve

Put the sun-dried tomatoes in a bowl, pour over the boiling water, and let stand for 5 minutes. Using a slotted spoon, remove one third of the tomatoes from the bowl. Cut into bite-size pieces. Put the remaining tomatoes and water into a blender and purée.

Heat the oil in a large skillet over medium heat. Add the onion and cook gently for 5 minutes, or until soft. Add the garlic and cook until just beginning to color. Add the puréed tomato and the reserved tomato pieces to the skillet. Bring to a boil, then simmer over medium–low heat for 10 minutes. Stir in the herbs and season to taste with salt and pepper. Simmer for 1 minute, then remove from the heat.

Bring a large saucepan of lightly salted water to a boil. Add the pasta, bring back to a boil, and cook for 8–10 minutes, or until tender but still firm to the bite. Drain and transfer to a warmed serving dish. Briefly reheat the sauce. Pour over the pasta, then add the basil and toss well to mix. Sprinkle with the Parmesan cheese and serve immediately.

Tagliatelle with Walnuts

serves 4

½ cup fresh white breadcrumbs

3 cups walnut pieces

2 garlic cloves, finely chopped

4 tbsp milk

4 tbsp olive oil

½ cup cream cheese

⅔ cup light cream

12 oz/350 g dried tagliatelle

salt and pepper

fresh flat-leaf parsley sprigs, to garnish

Place the breadcrumbs, walnuts, garlic, milk, oil, and cream cheese in a large mortar and grind to a smooth paste with a pestle. Alternatively, place the ingredients in a food processor and process until smooth. Stir in the cream to give a thick sauce consistency and season to taste with salt and pepper. Set aside.

Bring a large, heavy-bottom pan of lightly salted water to a boil. Add the pasta, return to a boil, and cook for 8–10 minutes, or until tender but still firm to the bite.

Drain the pasta and transfer to a warmed serving dish. Add the walnut sauce and toss thoroughly to coat. Garnish with parsley and serve immediately.

Pappardelle with Pumpkin Sauce

serves 4

4 tbsp butter

6 shallots, very finely chopped

1 lb 12 oz/800 g pumpkin, peeled, seeded, and cut into pieces

pinch of freshly grated nutmeg

3/4 cup light cream

4 tbsp freshly grated Parmesan cheese, plus extra to serve

2 tbsp chopped fresh flat-leaf parsley

12 oz/350 g dried pappardelle

salt

Melt the butter in a large, heavy-bottom pan. Add the shallots, sprinkle with a little salt, cover, and cook over very low heat, stirring occasionally, for 30 minutes.

Add the pumpkin pieces and season to taste with nutmeg. Cover and cook over very low heat, stirring occasionally, for 40 minutes, or until the pumpkin is pulpy. Stir in the cream, Parmesan cheese, and parsley, and remove the pan from the heat.

Meanwhile, bring a large, heavy-bottom pan of lightly salted water to a boil. Add the pasta, return to a boil, and cook for 8–10 minutes, or until tender but still firm to the bite. Drain, reserving 2–3 tablespoons of the cooking water.

Add the pasta to the pumpkin mixture and stir in the reserved cooking water if the mixture seems too thick. Cook, stirring constantly, for 1 minute, then transfer to a warmed serving dish and serve immediately with extra grated Parmesan cheese.

Tagliatelle with Garlic Crumbs

serves 4

6 cups fresh white breadcrumbs

4 tbsp finely chopped fresh flat-leaf parsley

1 tbsp chopped fresh chives

2 tbsp finely chopped fresh marjoram

3 tbsp olive oil, plus extra to serve

3–4 garlic cloves, finely chopped

½ cup pine nuts

1 lb/450 g dried tagliatelle

salt and pepper

½ cup freshly grated pecorino cheese, to serve

Mix the breadcrumbs, parsley, chives, and marjoram together in a small bowl. Heat the oil in a large heavy-bottom skillet. Add the breadcrumb mixture and the garlic and pine nuts, season to taste with salt and pepper, and cook over low heat, stirring constantly, for 5 minutes, or until the breadcrumbs become golden, but not crisp. Remove the skillet from the heat and cover to keep warm.

Bring a large heavy-bottom pan of lightly salted water to a boil. Add the pasta, return to a boil, and cook for 4–5 minutes, or until tender but still firm to the bite.

Drain the pasta and transfer to a warmed serving dish. Drizzle with oil to taste and toss to mix. Add the garlic breadcrumbs and toss again. Serve immediately with the pecorino cheese.

Linguine with Garlic & Bell Peppers

serves 4

6 large garlic cloves, unpeeled

14 oz/400 g bottled roasted red bell peppers, drained and sliced

7 oz/200 g canned chopped tomatoes

3 tbsp olive oil

1/4 tsp dried chile flakes

1 tsp chopped fresh oregano or thyme, plus extra sprigs to garnish

12 oz/350 g dried linguine

salt and pepper

Preheat the oven to 400°F/200°C. Place the unpeeled garlic cloves in a shallow, ovenproof dish. Roast in the preheated oven for 7–10 minutes, or until the garlic cloves feel soft.

Put the bell peppers, tomatoes, and oil in a food processor or blender, then purée. Squeeze the garlic flesh into the purée. Add the chile flakes and oregano. Season to taste with salt and pepper. Blend again, then scrape into a pan and set aside.

Bring a large saucepan of lightly salted water to a boil. Add the pasta, bring back to a boil, and cook for 8–10 minutes, or until tender but still firm to the bite. Drain and transfer to a warmed serving dish.

Reheat the sauce and pour over the pasta. Toss well to mix, garnish with oregano sprigs and serve immediately.

Fettuccine with Bell Peppers & Olives

serves 4

1/3 cup olive oil

1 onion, finely chopped

1 cup black olives, pitted and coarsely chopped

14 oz/400 g canned chopped tomatoes, drained

2 red, yellow, or orange bell peppers, seeded and cut into thin strips

12 oz/350 g dried fettuccine

salt and pepper

shavings of Romano cheese, to serve

Heat the oil in a large heavy-bottom pan. Add the onion and cook over low heat, stirring occasionally, for 5 minutes, or until softened. Add the olives, tomatoes, and bell peppers, and season to taste with salt and pepper. Cover and let simmer gently over very low heat, stirring occasionally, for 35 minutes.

Meanwhile, bring a large heavy-bottom pan of lightly salted water to a boil. Add the pasta, return to a boil, and cook for 8–10 minutes, or until tender but still firm to the bite. Drain the pasta and transfer to a warmed serving dish.

Spoon the sauce onto the pasta and toss well. Sprinkle generously with the Romano cheese and serve immediately.

Penne with Mixed Beans

serves 4

1 tbsp olive oil

1 onion, chopped

1 garlic clove, finely chopped

1 carrot, finely chopped

1 celery stalk, finely chopped

15 oz/425 g canned mixed beans, drained and rinsed

1 cup strained tomatoes

1 tbsp chopped fresh chervil, plus extra leaves to garnish

12 oz/350 g dried penne (pasta quills)

salt and pepper

Heat the oil in a large, heavy-bottom skillet. Add the onion, garlic, carrot, and celery, and cook over low heat, stirring occasionally, for 5 minutes, or until the onion has softened.

Add the mixed beans, strained tomatoes, and chopped chervil to the skillet and season the mixture to taste with salt and pepper. Cover and simmer gently for 15 minutes.

Meanwhile, bring a large, heavy-bottom pan of lightly salted water to a boil. Add the pasta, return to a boil, and cook for 8–10 minutes, or until tender but still firm to the bite. Drain the pasta and transfer to a warmed serving dish. Add the mixed bean sauce, toss well, and serve immediately, garnished with extra chervil.

anchovies
fettuccine with spinach & anchovies 91
linguine with bacon & olives 58
penne with Sicilian sauce 88
spaghetti alla puttanesca 86
spaghetti with tuna & parsley 92
apples: penne & apple salad 33
arugula
tagliatelle with smoked salmon & arugula 98
warm pasta salad 28
asparagus: penne with asparagus & Gorgonzola 135

bacon & ham
brown lentil & pasta soup 12
farfalle with Gorgonzola & ham 60
fusilli with bacon, eggs & mushrooms 54
linguine with bacon & olives 59
minestrone 10
pasta with bacon & tomatoes 56
penne with ham, tomato & chile 62
potato & pesto soup 16
saffron linguine 65
spaghetti alla carbonara 53
spaghetti bolognese 48
beans & pulses
brown lentil & pasta soup 12
chicken & bean soup 22
minestrone 10
penne with mixed beans 159
Tuscan bean soup 15
Tuscan veal broth 24
beef
rare beef pasta salad 36
spaghetti bolognese 48
spaghetti with meatballs 50
bell peppers
chicken & bean soup 22
farfalle with chicken & broccoli 80
fettuccine with bell peppers & olives 156
linguine with garlic & bell peppers 154
minestrone 10
pasta salad with bell peppers 34
pepperoni pasta 68
rigatoni with bell peppers & goat cheese 138
spicy sausage pasta salad 39
tagliatelle with creamy shrimp 106
tuna & fusilli salad 45
broccoli
creamy pappardelle & broccoli 132
farfalle with chicken & broccoli 80
fusilli with monkfish & broccoli 103

cabbage: minestrone 10
capers
Italian chicken spirals 83
sea bass with olive sauce 104
spaghetti alla puttanesca 86
celery
brown lentil & pasta soup 12
penne & apple salad 33
cheese
baked tuna & ricotta rigatoni 97
creamy pappardelle & broccoli 132
farfalle with Gorgonzola & ham 60
fusilli with bacon, eggs & mushrooms 54
fusilli with monkfish & broccoli 103
fusilli with ricotta, mint & garlic 136
pappardelle with pumpkin sauce 150
pasta salad with walnuts & Gorgonzola 30
penne with asparagus & Gorgonzola 135
penne with chicken & feta 78
rigatoni with bell peppers & goat cheese 138
spaghetti alla norma 142
tagliatelle with walnuts 148
tagliatelle with wild mushrooms & mascarpone 141
chicken
chicken & bean soup 22
chicken with creamy penne 74
farfalle with chicken & broccoli 80
Italian chicken soup 21
Italian chicken spirals 83
penne with chicken & feta 78
spaghetti with parsley chicken 77
clams
Neapolitan seafood salad 42
spaghetti con vongole 116
corn: Italian chicken soup 21
crab: spaghetti with crab 118

eggplant: spaghetti alla norma 142
eggs
fusilli with bacon, eggs & mushrooms 54
spaghetti alla carbonara 53

garlic
fettuccine with garlic, tomatoes & olives 130
fusilli with ricotta, mint & garlic 136
linguine with garlic & bell peppers 154
spaghetti olio e aglio 129
tagliatelle with garlic crumbs 153

lamb: pasticcio 72

melon: pasta salad with melon & shrimp 40
minestrone 10
monkfish
fish soup with macaroni 27
fusilli with monkfish & broccoli 103
mushrooms
farfalle with Gorgonzola & ham 60
fusilli with bacon, eggs & mushrooms 54
linguine with bacon & olives 59
pappardelle with scallops & porcini mushrooms 112
rigatoni with chorizo & mushrooms 71
spaghettini with quick tuna sauce 94
tagliatelle with wild mushrooms & mascarpone 141
mussels
fish soup with macaroni 27
Neapolitan seafood salad 42

nuts
fettuccine with spinach & anchovies 91
Italian chicken spirals 83
macaroni with scallops & pine nuts 115
pasta salad with walnuts & Gorgonzola 30
penne & apple salad 33
penne with Sicilian sauce 88
tagliatelle with walnuts 148
tagliatelle with garlic crumbs 153
tagliatelle with pesto 126

olives
fettuccine with bell peppers & olives 156
fettuccine with garlic, tomatoes & olives 130
Italian chicken spirals 83
linguine with bacon & olives 59
rigatoni with bell peppers & goat cheese 138
sea bass with olive sauce 104
spaghetti alla puttanesca 86

peas
chicken with creamy penne 74
fusilli with shrimp & peas 109
minestrone 10
pesto
pasta salad with bell peppers 34
potato & pesto soup 16
tagliatelle with pesto 126
potato & pesto soup 16
pumpkin: pappardelle with pumpkin sauce 150

saffron linguine 65
salad, warm pasta 28
sausage
penne with sausage sauce 66
pepperoni pasta 68
rigatoni with chorizo & mushrooms 71
spicy sausage pasta salad 39
scallops
linguine with shrimp & scallops 110
macaroni with scallops & pine nuts 115
pappardelle with scallops & porcini mushrooms 112
sea bass with olive sauce 104
shrimp
fish soup with macaroni 27
fusilli with shrimp & peas 109
linguine with shrimp & scallops 110
pasta salad with melon & shrimp 40
tagliatelle with creamy shrimp 106
smoked salmon
conchiglie with smoked salmon & sour cream 100
tagliatelle with smoked salmon & arugula 98
spinach: fettuccine with spinach & anchovies 91
squid
Neapolitan seafood salad 42
penne with squid & tomatoes 121

tomatoes
baked tuna & ricotta rigatoni 97
fettuccine with bell peppers & olives 156
fettuccine with garlic, tomatoes & olives 130
fish soup with macaroni 27
fresh tomato soup 18
fusilli with sun-dried tomatoes 147
Italian chicken spirals 83
linguine with garlic & bell peppers 154
minestrone 10
pasta with bacon & tomatoes 56
penne with ham, tomato & chile 62
penne with mixed beans 159
penne with sausage sauce 66
penne with Sicilian sauce 88
penne with squid & tomatoes 121
pepperoni pasta 68
rare beef pasta salad 36
spaghetti alla norma 142
spaghetti alla puttanesca 86
spaghetti bolognese 48
spaghetti with meatballs 50
spaghetti with tomato & basil 124
spaghettini with quick tuna sauce 94
Tuscan veal broth 24
warm pasta salad 28
tuna
baked tuna & ricotta rigatoni 97
spaghetti with tuna & parsley 92
spaghettini with quick tuna sauce 94
tuna & fusilli salad 45

veal: Tuscan veal broth 24

zucchini: fusilli with zucchini & lemon 144